the FIRE *of* LOVE

the FIRE *of* LOVE

Meditations on Following Christ Wholeheartedly

THOMAS À KEMPIS

WHITAKER
HOUSE

Publisher's note: All quotations in this book, lightly edited, are taken from Thomas à Kempis, *The Imitation of Christ* (New Kensington, PA: Whitaker House, 1981, 2025), which was updated for the modern reader; words, expressions, and sentence structure were revised for clarity and readability.

All Scripture quotations are taken from the King James Version of the Holy Bible.

The Fire of Love:
Meditations on Following Christ Wholeheartedly

ISBN: 979-8-88769-622-5
eBook ISBN: 979-8-88769-623-2
Printed in Colombia

Whitaker House
1030 Hunt Valley Circle
New Kensington, PA 15068
www.whitakerhouse.com

Library of Congress Control Number: 2025946712

1 2 3 4 5 6 7 8 9 10 11 **W** 33 32 31 30 29 28 27 26

Refresh Your hungry beggar,
inflame my coldness with the fire of Your love,
enlighten my blindness with
the brightness of Your presence.

—Thomas à Kempis

About Thomas à Kempis and *The Fire of Love*

Thomas à Kempis (1379–1471) was a German monk who emphasized withdrawal from the attractions of the world. Born in the Rhineland town of Kempen, he attended a school at nearby Deventer in Holland that had been started by Gerard Groote, founder of the Brothers of the Common Life. These were men devoted to prayer, simplicity, and union with God. When Thomas was nineteen, he entered the monastery of Mount St. Agnes, which the brothers had recently started near Zwolle in Holland. He spent the rest of his long life behind the walls of that monastery.

Thomas devoted himself to prayer, study, copying manuscripts, teaching novices, offering Mass, and hearing the confessions of people who came to the monastery church. He wrote a number of sermons, letters, hymns, and information about the lives of the saints. Thomas is most famous for *The Imitation of Christ,* a little instruction book on how to love God. *The Imitation,* beloved by Christians for centuries, is said to be the most widely read devotional work next to the Bible. In its pages, the author urges his readers to give themselves fully to God and to wholeheartedly follow Christ, becoming more like Him each day.

The Fire of Love: Meditations on Following Christ Wholeheartedly is filled with specially chosen quotations from this renowned spiritual book.

In the *Imitation,* Thomas à Kempis talks about the "fire of love," referring to both the fire of God's love filling us and burning off the chaff of our lives, and the fire of our increasingly devoted love for Him, such as in these prayers he offers to God:

> Lord, I offer unto You, on Your propitiatory altar, all my sins and offenses, which I have committed before You and Your holy angels, from the day wherein I first could sin even to this hour; that You may consume and burn them, one and all, with the fire of Your love, and blot out all the stains of my sins, and cleanse my conscience from every offense, and restore to me Your grace, which by sinning I lost, fully forgiving me all and admitting me mercifully to the kiss of peace.

> What marvel is it if I should be wholly on fire from You and of myself fail and come to nothing; since You are Fire always burning and never failing, Love purifying the heart, and enlightening the understanding!

> I…wish to be on fire with great and holy desires, and to offer myself up to You from my whole heart.

As you read and meditate on the excerpts in this book, may you be inspired to pursue greater love, devotion, and service for God. May you, like Thomas à Kempis, allow God to kindle a flame within you to be devoted to Him above all else and to wholeheartedly imitate the life of His Son, the Lord Jesus Christ. As Kempis expressed:

> Who is there that, approaching humbly unto a fountain of sweetness, does not carry away some little sweetness? Or who, standing near a great fire, receives not some small heat therefrom? And You are a fountain always full and overflowing; a fire ever burning and never going out. Wherefore, if I am not permitted to draw out of the fullness of the fountain, nor to drink my fill, I will, notwithstanding, set my lips to the mouth of this heavenly conduit, that I may receive from thence at least some small drop to refresh my thirst and may not wither. And though I cannot as yet be altogether heavenly, nor so on fire as the cherubim and seraphim, yet, notwithstanding, I will endeavor to apply myself earnestly to devotion and to prepare my heart to obtain but some small flame of divine fire.

"Send out thy light and thy truth" (Psalm 43:3), that they may shine upon the earth; for I am earth without form and void until You enlighten me. Pour forth Your grace from above, shower upon my heart the dew of heaven, supply fresh streams of devotion to water the face of the earth, that it may bring forth good and excellent fruit.

Blessed are the ears that catch the pulses of the divine whisper and give no heed to the whisperings of this world. Blessed indeed are those ears that listen not after the voice sounding without but for the truth teaching inwardly.

O God, who are the Truth,
make me one with You in continual love!

"He that followeth me shall not walk in darkness" (John 8:12), says the Lord. These are the words of Christ by which we are admonished how we ought to imitate His life and manners, if we would be enlightened and delivered from all blindness of heart. Let therefore our chief endeavor be to meditate upon the life of Jesus Christ.

Whosoever will fully and with relish understand the words of Christ must endeavor to conform his life wholly to the life of Christ.

The doctrine of Christ exceeds all the doctrine of holy men, and he who has the Spirit will find therein *"the hidden manna"* (Revelation 2:17).

He who embraces Jesus shall be made strong forever.

He who finds Jesus finds a good treasure, yes, a Good above all good. And he who loses Jesus loses much indeed, more than the whole world! Poor is he who lives without Jesus; and rich is he who is well with Jesus.

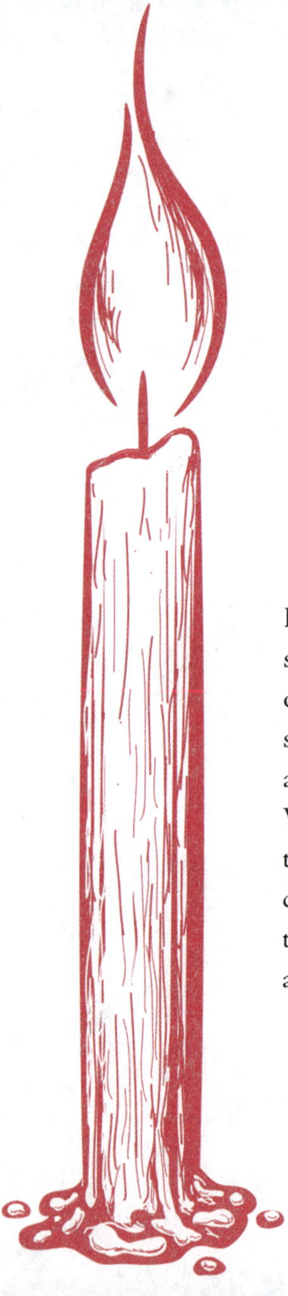

He to whom the eternal Word speaks is set free from many opinions. From that one Word are all things, and all things speak; and this is the Beginning, which also speaks to us. No man without that Word understands or judges rightly. He to whom all things are one, and who draws all things to one, and sees all things in one, can be steadfast in heart and peaceably repose in God.

In silence and in stillness, a devout soul profits and learns the hidden things of the Scriptures.

You did first stir me up that I might seek You. Blessed be You therefore, O Lord, that have shown this goodness to Your servant, according to the multitude of Your mercies.

Glory not in wealth if you have it, nor in friends because they are powerful, but in God who gives all things and, above all, desires to give you Himself.

By two wings a man is lifted up from things earthly,
namely, by simplicity and purity.
Simplicity ought to be in our intention;
purity in our affection.
Simplicity tends toward God;
purity apprehends and tastes Him.

They [the prophets] may indeed sound forth words, but they cannot give the Spirit. Beautiful is their speech, but if You be silent, they kindle not the heart.... They declare commandments, but You help us to fulfill them. They point out the way, but You give strength to walk in it. They work only from without, but You instruct and enlighten hearts. They water outwardly, but You give the increase. They cry aloud in words, but You to the hearing impart understanding.

All perfection in this life has some imperfection bound up with it, and no knowledge of ours is without some darkness. A humble knowledge of self is a surer way to God than a deep search after learning. Yet learning is not to be blamed, nor the mere knowledge of anything whatsoever, for knowledge is good, considered in itself, and ordained by God; but a good conscience and a virtuous life are always to be preferred before it. But because many endeavor rather to know than to live well, therefore they are often deceived and reap either none or scanty fruit.

He is truly great who is great in love.

He is truly great who is little in himself and who makes no account of any height of honor. He is truly wise who accounts all earthly things "*but dung, that* [he] *may win Christ*" (Philippians 3:8). He is truly very learned who does the will of God and forsakes his own will.

God weighs more the love
out of which a man works
than the work that he does.
He does much who loves much.
He does much who does a thing well.

We must diligently search
into and set in order both
the outward and the inner man
because both of them are
of importance to our progress in godliness.

Shut your door and call unto Jesus, your Beloved.
Stay with Him in your closet,
for you shall not find elsewhere so great a peace.

The humbler a man is in himself, and the more resigned to God, the more prudent will he be in all things, and the more at peace.

True peace of heart…is found by resisting our passions, not by obeying them. There is then no peace in the heart of a carnal man, nor in him who is given up to outward things, but in the fervent and spiritual man.

Blessed are the single-hearted,
for they shall enjoy much peace.

God wills us to be perfectly subject to Him, and, by the fire of love, to transcend all human reason.

Who is so wise that he can fully know all things?
Be not therefore too confident in
your own mind but be
willing to hear the minds of others.

Each one's opinion may be good;
but to refuse to yield to others
when reason or a special cause requires
it is a sign of pride and obstinacy.

*Gather some profit wherever you are so that,
if you see or hear any good examples,
you can kindle yourself to the imitation thereof.*

Endeavor to be patient in bearing with the defects and infirmities of others, of whatever sort they be, for you also have many failings that must be borne with by others. If you cannot make yourself such a one as you would, how will you be able to have another in all things to your liking?

If you will withdraw yourself from speaking vainly
and from gabbing idly,
as also from hearkening after new things and rumors,
you shall find enough suitable time
for meditation on good things.

When one who was in anxiety of mind, often wavering between fear and hope, did once, being overcome with grief, prostrate himself in a church before a certain altar in prayer, and pondered thus within himself, saying, "Oh, if I knew that I should yet persevere!" he presently heard within him a divine answer: "If you did know this, what would you do? Do now what you would do then, and you shall be perfectly secure." And being thus comforted and strengthened, he committed himself wholly to the divine will, and that anxious tossing ceased. And he willed not to search curiously, to know what things should befall him, but rather labored to seek out what was the acceptable and perfect will of God for the beginning and the accomplishing of every good work.

He stands
very unsteadily
who casts not
all his anxiety
upon You.

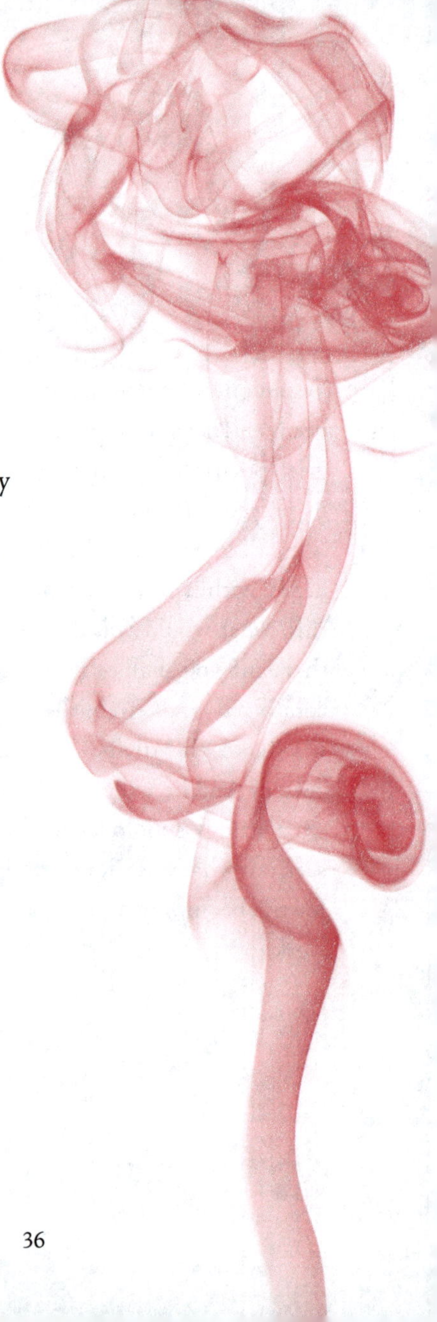

When a man comes to that state where he seeks not his comfort from any creature, then God first begins to be altogether sweet to him. Then shall he be contented with whatever befalls him in this world. Then shall he neither rejoice in great matters nor be sorrowful for small, but entirely and confidently he commits himself to God, who is unto him all in all, to whom assuredly nothing perishes or dies, but all things do live unto Him and serve Him without delay.

God protects the humble and delivers him. He loves and comforts the humble; unto the humble man He inclines Himself; unto the humble He gives great grace; and after his humiliation He raises him to glory. Unto the humble He reveals His secrets and sweetly draws and invites him unto Himself.

[God says,] "All is not lost, although you feel yourself very often afflicted or grievously tempted. You are a man, and not God; you are flesh, not an angel. How could you continue always in the same state of virtue when an angel in heaven has failed in this, as also the first man in the garden of Eden? I am He who lifts up the mourners to safety and soundness, and those who know their own weakness I advance to My own divine nature."

God alone is everlasting and of infinite greatness,
filling all things, the soul's solace
and the true joy of the heart.

Oh, that nothing else lay upon us
to do but with our mouth
and whole heart to
praise our Lord God!

Sweetly enough he rides whom the grace of God carries. And what marvel if he does not feel his burden, who is borne up by the Almighty and led by the Sovereign Guide?

Not all that is high is holy;
nor all that is sweet, good;
nor every desire, pure;
nor is everything that is dear
unto us pleasing to God.
Willingly do I accept of that grace
whereby I may ever be found
more humble and more fearful
and may become readier to
renounce myself.

All the servants of the cross,
who in their lifetime conformed themselves
unto Christ crucified,
shall draw near unto Christ
the judge with great confidence.
Why therefore fear to take up the cross
that leads to a kingdom?

In the cross is salvation, in the cross is life, in the cross is protection against our enemies, in the cross is infusion of heavenly sweetness, in the cross is strength of mind, in the cross is joy of spirit, in the cross is the height of virtue, in the cross is the perfection of holiness. There is no salvation of the soul, or hope of everlasting life, but in the cross. Take up therefore your cross and follow Jesus, and you shall go into life everlasting.

There is no other way unto life and unto true inward peace but the way of the cross and of daily mortification. Walk where you will, seek whatever you will, you shall not find a higher way above, nor a safer way below, than the way of the cross.

Keep this short and perfect word:
Let go all, and you shall find all;
leave desire, and you shall find rest.
Weigh this thoroughly in your mind,
and when you have fulfilled it,
you shall understand all things.

Thus says your Beloved,
"I am your Salvation, your Peace, and your Life:
keep yourself with Me, and you shall find peace.
Let go all transitory things and seek the things eternal."

[God says,]
"The world promises things temporal and mean,
and is served with great eagerness.
I promise things most high and eternal,
and the hearts of mortals grow dull.
Who is there that in all things serves and obeys
Me with so great care as the world
and its lords are served withal?"

Nothing is sweeter than love, nothing stronger, nothing higher, nothing wider, nothing more pleasant, nothing fuller or better in heaven and earth; because love is born of God and cannot rest but in God, above all created things. A lover flies, runs, and rejoices; he is free and is not bound. He gives all for all and has all in all, because he rests in One highest above all things, from whom all that is good flows.

This is the work of Your love, freely keeping me and relieving me in so many necessities, guarding me also from pressing dangers and snatching me (as I may truly say) from evils without number.

By loving myself amiss,
I lost myself;
and seeking You alone
and purely loving You,
I have found both
myself and You.

I...wish to be on fire
with great and holy desires,
and to offer myself up
to You from my whole heart.

Truly unspeakable is the sweetness of contemplating You, which You bestow on them who love You. In this, especially, You have shown me the sweetness of Your love—that when I was not, You made me; when I went far astray from You, You brought me back again, that I might serve You, and You have commanded me to love You.

Fountain of love unceasing,
what shall I say concerning You?
How can I forget You,
who have vouchsafed to remember me,
even after I had wasted away and perished?
You have shown mercy to Your servant
beyond all hope and have exhibited favor
and loving-kindness beyond all desert.

"Let not your heart be troubled, neither let it be afraid" (John 14:27). Trust in Me, and have confidence in My mercy. When you think yourself far from Me, oftentimes I am the nearest. When you count almost all to be lost, then oftentimes the greater gain of reward is close at hand. All is not lost when anything falls out contrary. You ought not to judge according to present feeling, nor to take any heaviness or give yourself over to it, from wherever it comes, as though all hope of rising therefrom were taken away. Think not yourself wholly left, although for a time I have sent some tribulation or even have withdrawn desired comfort; for this is the passage to the kingdom of heaven.

O Lord, how entirely needful is Your grace for me to begin anything good, to proceed with it, and to accomplish it. For without it, I can do nothing, but in You, I can do all things when Your grace strengthens me....

Grace makes the poor in spirit rich in virtues and renders him who is rich in many goods humble in heart. Come down to me, O Lord, come and in the morning fill me with Your comfort, lest my soul faint for weariness and dryness of mind!

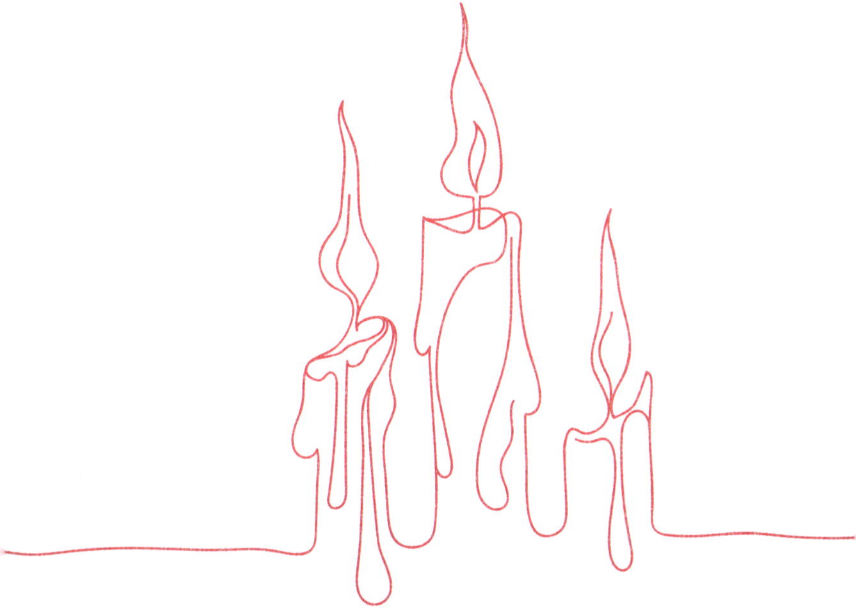

Everlasting Light, surpassing all created luminaries, "*cast forth lightning*" (Psalm 144:6) from above, piercing all the most inward parts of my heart. Make clean, make glad, make bright, and make alive my spirit with all the powers thereof, that I may cleave unto You in ecstasies of joy. When will that blessed and desired hour come, that You may satisfy me with Your presence and be unto me all in all!

Your grace is the mistress of truth, the teacher of discipline, the light of the heart, the solace of affliction, the driver-away of sorrow, the expeller of fear, the nurse of devotion, the source and fountain of tears.

My son, says the Lord,
the more you can go out of yourself,
the more will you be able to enter into Me.

Follow Me:
"I am the way, the truth, and the life"
(John 14:6).

Without the Way, there is no going; without the Truth, there is no knowing; without the Life, there is no living. I am the Way, which you ought to follow; the Truth, which you ought to believe; the Life, which you ought to hope for. I am the Way inviolable, the Truth infallible, the Life unending. I am the Way that is straightest, the Truth that is highest, the Life that is truest, the Life blessed, the Life uncreated. If you remain in My way, *"ye shall know the truth, and the truth shall make you free"* (John 8:32), and you shall lay hold on eternal life.

What do I require more than that you study to resign yourself entirely to Me? Whatever you give besides yourself, I regard not; for I seek not your gift but you. As it would not satisfy you to have all things without Me, so neither can it please Me, whatever you give, if you offer not yourself. Offer up yourself to Me, and give yourself wholly for God, and your offering shall be accepted. Behold, I offered up Myself wholly unto My Father for you. I gave also My whole body and blood for you, that I might be wholly yours, and that you might continue to be Mine to the end. But if you stand upon yourself and do not offer yourself up freely to My will, the offering is not complete, neither will there be entire union between us.

What creature under heaven is there so beloved as the devout soul into which God Himself enters?

O unspeakable grace! O wondrous condescension! O unmeasurable love bestowed on man!

But what return shall I make to the Lord for this grace, for love so unparalleled? There is nothing else that I am able to present more acceptable than to offer my heart wholly to my God and to unite it most inwardly unto Him.

Then shall all my inward parts rejoice, when my soul shall be perfectly made one with God. Then will He say unto me, "If you are willing to be with Me, I am willing to be with you." And I will answer Him, "Vouchsafe, O Lord, to remain with me; I will gladly be with You. This is my whole desire, that my heart be made one with You."

Lord Jesus,
how great is the pleasure of the devout soul
that feasts with You in Your banquet,
where there is set no other food to be eaten but Yourself,
the only Beloved and most to be desired
above all the desires of the heart!

Lord, I offer unto You, on Your propitiatory altar, all my sins and offenses, which I have committed before You and Your holy angels from the day wherein I first could sin even to this hour; that You may consume and burn them, one and all, with the fire of Your love, and blot out all the stains of my sins, and cleanse my conscience from every offense, and restore to me Your grace, which by sinning I lost, fully forgiving me all and admitting me mercifully to the kiss of peace.

Oh, that with Your presence You would wholly inflame, consume, and transform me into Yourself, that I might be made one Spirit with You by the grace of inward union and by the meltings of ardent love! Suffer me not to go away from You hungry and dry, but deal mercifully with me, as oftentimes You have dealt wonderfully with Your saints. What marvel is it if I should be wholly on fire from You and of myself fail and come to nothing; since You are Fire always burning and never failing, Love purifying the heart and enlightening the understanding!

Let me sing the song of love. Let me follow You, my Beloved, on high. Let my soul spend itself in Your praise, rejoicing through love. Let me love You more than myself, nor love myself but for You; and in You all that truly love You, as the law of love commands, shining out from Yourself.

Love is swift, sincere, kindly affectioned,
pleasant, and delightsome; brave, patient,
faithful, prudent, long-suffering, strong,
and never seeking itself.
For where a person seeks himself,
there he falls from love.

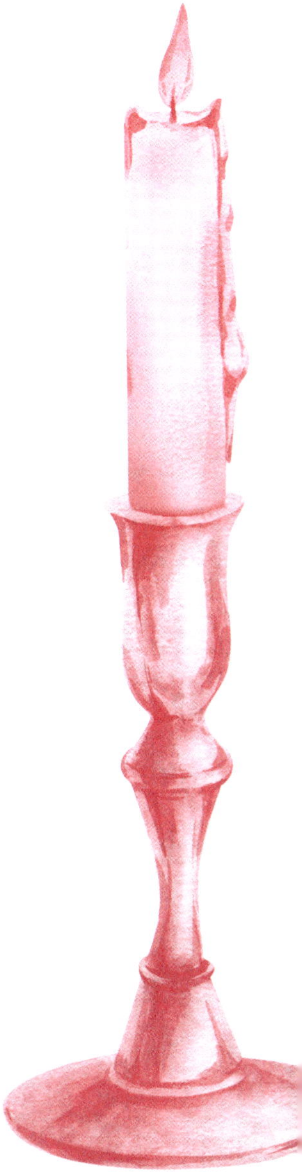

Love is circumspect, humble, and upright;
not yielding to softness, or to lightness,
nor attending to vain things.
It is sober, chaste, firm, quiet, and guarded in all the senses.

He that is not prepared to suffer all things and to do the will of his Beloved is not worthy to be called a lover. A lover ought to embrace willingly all that is hard and bitter, for the sake of his Beloved, nor to turn away from Him for things that fall out against one.

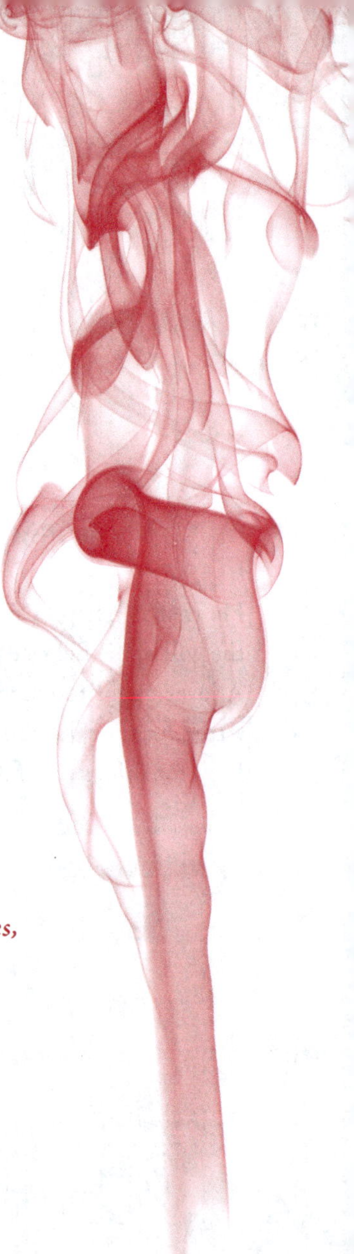

*Truly, when the day of judgment comes,
we shall not be examined by what we
have read but by what we have done;
not by how well we have spoken
but by how we have lived.*

You, O Lord my God, are above all things the best; You alone are most high, You alone most powerful, You alone most sufficient and most full, You alone most sweet and most full of consolation. You alone are most lovely and loving, You alone most noble and glorious above all things; in whom all good things together both perfectly are, and ever have been, and shall be. And, therefore, it is too small and unsatisfying, whatever You bestow on me besides Yourself, or reveal unto me of Yourself, or promise, while You are not seen nor fully obtained. For surely my heart cannot truly rest nor be entirely contented unless it rest in You and surmount all gifts and every creature.

O most beloved Bridegroom of my soul,
Jesus Christ,
the most pure Lover,
the Lord of all creation,
who will give me the wings of true liberty,
that I might flee away and rest in You!

As iron put into the fire loses its rust and becomes altogether white and glowing, so is he who wholly turns himself unto God, puts off all slothfulness, and is transformed into a new man. When a man begins to grow lukewarm, then he is afraid of small labor and willingly receives outward comfort. But when he once begins to overcome himself perfectly and to walk boldly in the way of God, then he esteems those things less that before were grievous unto him.

The more a man is at one within himself and becomes single in heart, so much the more and higher things does he understand without labor, for he receives the light of understanding from above. A pure, sincere, and stable spirit is not distracted in a multitude of affairs, for it works all to the honor of God and inwardly strives to be at rest from all self-seeking.

You cannot be fully comforted, nor have perfect refreshment, except in God, the Comforter of the poor and Patron of the humble. Wait a little while, O my soul, wait for the divine promise, and you shall have abundance of all good things in heaven.

How great thanks am I bound to render unto You that You have vouchsafed to show unto me and to all faithful people the good and the right way to Your eternal kingdom! For Your life is our way, and, by holy patience, we walk toward You who are our Crown. If You had not gone before us and taught us, who would care to follow? Alas, how many would remain behind and afar off if they did not gaze upon Your glorious example! Behold, even yet we are lukewarm, though we have heard of so many of Your miracles and teachings. What would become of us if we had not so great light whereby to follow You!

Lord, let that become possible to me
by grace which by nature seems
to me impossible! You know that I am
able to suffer but little and that
I am quickly cast down when
a slight adversity arises.
For Your name's sake,
let every exercise of tribulation
be made lovable and desirable to me;
for to suffer and to be disquieted
for Your sake is
very wholesome for my soul.

Above all things and in all things, O my soul, rest in the Lord always, for He is the everlasting rest of the saints.

Grant me, O loving Jesus, to rest in You above every creature: above all health and beauty, above all glory and honor, above all power and dignity, above all knowledge and subtlety, above all riches and arts, above all joy and gladness, above all fame and praise, above all sweetness and comfort, above all hope and promise, above all desert and desire. Above all gifts and favors that You can give and pour upon us, above all mirth and exultation that the mind can receive and feel; finally, above all—above angels and archangels, and above all the host of heaven, above all things visible and invisible, and above all that is not You, my God.

Behold, here I am! Behold,
I come unto you, because you have called upon Me!
Your tears and the desire of your soul,
your humiliation and your contrition of heart,
have inclined and brought Me unto you.

There is none like unto You
in all the wonderful things
of heaven and earth.
Your works are very good,
Your judgments true,
and by Your providence
the universe is ruled.
Praise therefore and glory be
unto You, O wisdom of the Father;
let my mouth, my soul,
and all created things together
praise and bless You.

All that we have in soul and in body, and whatever we possess outwardly or inwardly, by nature or beyond nature, are Your benefits and proclaim You bountiful, merciful, and good, from whom we have received all good things.

Although one has received more, another less, all notwithstanding are Yours, and without You even the least blessing cannot be had.

[God says,] "There are some who resign themselves but with certain exceptions. They put not their full trust in God, and therefore they study how to provide for themselves. Some also, at first, offer all, but afterward being assailed with temptation, they return again to their own ways, and therefore make no progress in the path of virtue. These shall not attain to the true liberty of a pure heart, nor to the favor of sweet familiarity with Me, unless they first make an entire resignation and a daily sacrifice of themselves. Without this, no union that bears fruit stands firm nor shall stand."

"O God, be not far from me: O my God, make haste for my help" (Psalm 71:12). For there have risen up against me many thoughts and great fears, afflicting my soul. How shall I pass through unhurt? How shall I break them to pieces?

He says, *"I will go before thee, and make the crooked places straight:...I will give thee the treasures of darkness, and hidden riches of secret places"* (Isaiah 45:2–3).

Do, O Lord, as You say, and let all evil thoughts fly from before Your face. This is my hope, my only consolation, to flee unto You from my inmost heart and to wait patiently for Your consolation.

Lord Jesus, enlighten me with the clear shining of an inward light, and remove all darkness from the habitation of my heart. Repress my many wandering thoughts, and break in pieces those temptations that violently assault me. Fight strongly for me and vanquish the evil beasts, the alluring desires of the flesh, so there may be peace in Your walls and that Your abundant praise may resound in Your holy court, that is, in a pure conscience. Command the winds and tempests; say unto the sea, Be still; say to the north wind, Blow not; and there shall be a great calm.

Let this be your endeavor,
this your prayer, this your desire,
that you may be stripped
of all selfishness and,
naked, follow the naked Jesus;
may die to self and live eternally to Me.
Then shall fail all vain imaginations,
evil perturbations, and superfluous cares.
Then also immoderate fear shall depart,
and inordinate love shall die.

Love all for Jesus, but Jesus for Himself.
Jesus Christ alone is singularly to be beloved.
He alone is found good and faithful above all friends.
For Him and in Him, let both friends and foes be dear unto you.
And all these are to be prayed for,
that He would make them all to know and love Him.

When Jesus speaks not inwardly to us, all other comfort is worth nothing; but if Jesus speaks but one word, we feel great comfort. Did not Mary rise immediately from the place where she wept when Martha said to her, "*The Master is come, and calleth for thee*" (John 11:28)? Happy hour when Jesus calls from tears to spiritual joy!

He has great tranquility of heart who cares neither for the praises nor the faultfinding of men. He will easily be content and pacified whose conscience is pure. You are not holier if you are praised, nor the more worthless if you are found to be with fault. What you are, that you are; neither by words can you be made greater than what you are in the sight of God.

If you consider what you are within, you will not care what men say of you. Man looks on the countenance, but God on the heart. Man considers the deeds, but God weighs the intentions.

How seldom
we weigh our neighbor in
the same balance
with ourselves.

Count it not of great importance who is for you or against you, but let this be your aim and care: that God be with you in everything you do. Have a good conscience, and God shall defend you. For whom God wills to help, no man's perverseness shall be able to hurt. If you know how to be silent and suffer, without doubt you shall see the help of the Lord. He Himself knows the time and manner of delivering you, and therefore you ought to resign yourself unto Him. It belongs to God to help and to deliver from all confusion.

My son, says the Lord, you ought with all diligence to work toward this, that in every place and in every external action or occupation, you may be inwardly free and thoroughly master of yourself. That all things be under you and not you under them; that you be lord and master of your own actions, not a slave or a hireling. Rather, you should be as a freed man and a true Hebrew, passing over into the lot and freedom of the sons of God; who stand upon things present and contemplate things eternal; who look on transitory things with the left eye and with the right on the things of heaven; whom temporal things draw not to cleave unto them. Rather, they draw temporal things to serve them well, in such ways as they are ordained by God and appointed by the great Workmaster, who has left nothing in His creation without due order.

If, too, in every event you stand not on the outside, nor with a carnal eye survey things seen or heard, but in every affair enter with Moses into the tabernacle to ask counsel of the Lord, you shall sometimes hear the Divine Oracle and shall return instructed concerning many things, both present and to come. For Moses always had recourse to the tabernacle for the dissolving of doubts and questions and fled to the help of prayer for support under dangers and the iniquity of men. So ought you, in like manner, take refuge within the closet of your heart, earnestly seeking the divine favor.

The perfect victory is to triumph over ourselves.
For he who keeps himself subject,
that his sensual affections be obedient to reason,
and his reason in all things obedient to Me,
that person is truly conqueror of himself and lord of the world.

*Be not ashamed
to serve others
for the love of
Jesus Christ,
nor to be esteemed
poor in this world.
Presume not
upon yourself,
but place
your hope
in God.
Do what
lies in you,
and God will
assist your
good will.*

Grant me, O Lord,
to know that which is worth knowing,
to love that which is worth loving,
to praise that which pleases You most,
to esteem that which to You seems precious,
to abhor that which in Your sight is unclean.

You came to serve, not to rule. Know that you were called to suffer and to labor, not to be idle and spend your time in talk. Here therefore men are proved as gold in the furnace. Here no man can stand, unless he be willing to humble himself with his whole heart for the love of God.

Never be entirely idle,
but either be reading,
or writing, or praying,
or meditating,
or endeavoring something
for the public good.

The saints of God and all the devout friends of Christ regarded not those things that pleased the flesh, nor those that flourished in this present time, but all their hope and endeavor panted after the good things that are eternal. Their whole desire was carried upward to things durable and invisible, that the desire of things visible might not draw them to things below.

How wise and happy is he who now labors to be in life as he wishes to be found at his death! A perfect contempt of the world, a fervent desire to go forward in virtue, the love of discipline, the painfulness of repentance, the readiness of obedience, the denying of ourselves, and the bearing of any adversity whatever for the love of Christ will give us great confidence that we shall die happily.

You have good cause to be ashamed in looking upon the life of Jesus Christ, seeing you have not as yet endeavored to conform yourself more unto Him, though you have been a long time in the way of God. A religious person who exercises himself seriously and devoutly in the most holy life and passion of our Lord shall there abundantly find whatever is profitable and necessary for him, neither shall he need to seek any better thing besides Jesus. Oh, if Jesus crucified would come into our hearts, how quickly and fully would we be taught!

Christ will come to you and show you His consolation if you prepare for Him a worthy abode within. All His glory and beauty are from within, and there He delights Himself.

He often visits the inward man and has sweet discourse, pleasant solace, much peace, and familiarity exceedingly wonderful with him.

O faithful soul, make ready your heart for this Bridegroom, that He may vouchsafe to come and dwell within you! For thus says He: "*If a man love me, he will keep my words..., and we will come unto him, and make our abode with him*" (John 14:23).

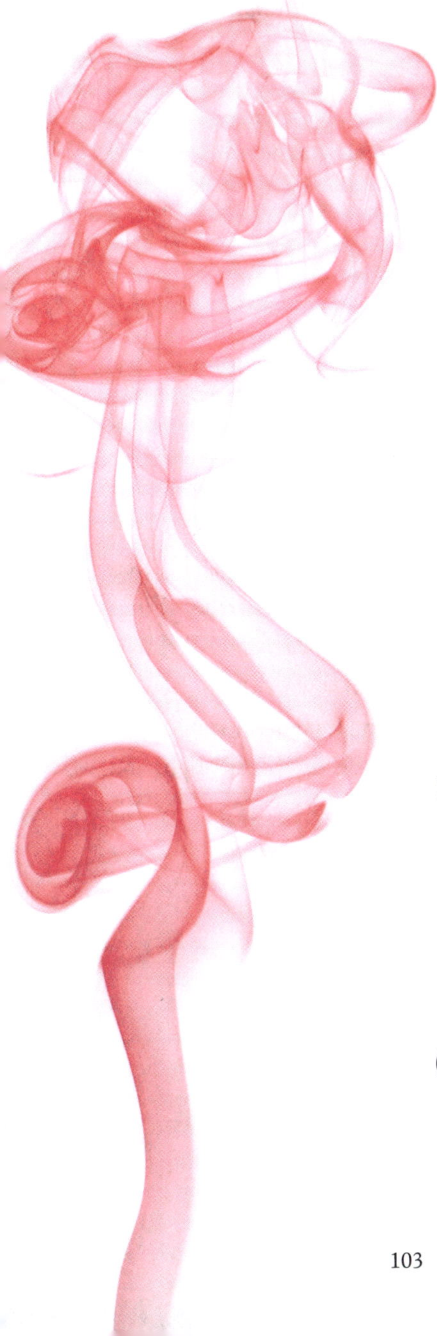

When you have Christ,
you are rich and have enough.
He Himself will be your
provider and faithful steward
in all things so that you need
not trust in men. For men
soon change and quickly fail,
but *"Christ abideth for ever"*
(John 12:34) and stands by us
firmly unto the end.

Neither shall you ever have rest unless you be most inwardly united unto Christ. Why do you here look about since this is not the place of your rest? Heaven ought to be your dwelling place, and all earthly things are to be looked upon as it were by the way. All things are passing away, and you together with them. Beware that you do not cleave unto them, lest you be caught and perish. Let your meditation be on the Most High, and your prayer for mercy be directed unto

Christ without ceasing.

Remain in some secret place, and enjoy your God; for you have Him, whom all the world cannot take from you. I am He, to whom you ought wholly to give up yourself, that you may now live no longer in yourself but in Me, free from all anxiety of mind.

According to our purpose shall be the course of our spiritual profiting; and much diligence is necessary to him who will profit much. And if he who firmly purposes often fails, what shall he do who seldom, or with little firmness, purposes anything? It turns out in various ways that we leave off our purpose; yet the light omission of spiritual exercises seldom passes without some loss to our souls. The purpose of just men depends not upon their own wisdom but upon God's grace, on whom too they always rely for whatever they take in hand. For man proposes but God disposes; neither is the way of man in himself.

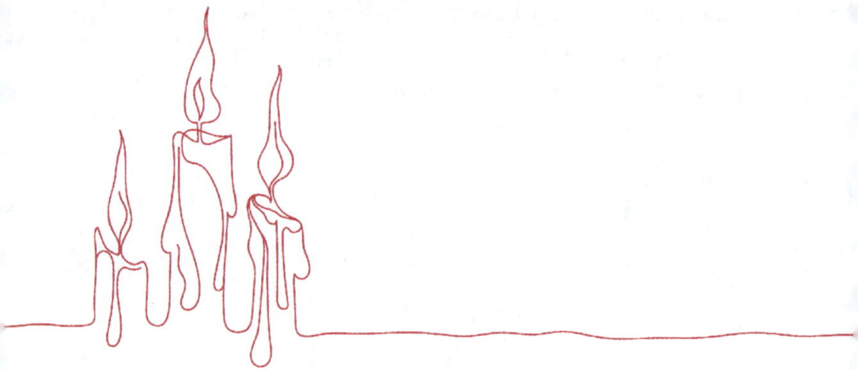

Love often knows no measure but is fervent beyond all measure. Love feels no burden, thinks nothing of labors, attempts what is above its strength, pleads no excuse of impossibility; for it thinks all things possible for itself and all things lawful. It is therefore strong for all things, and it completes many things and brings them to effect, where he who does not love faints and lies down. Love is watchful, and sleeping slumbers not. Though wearied, it is not tired; though pressed, it is not in straits; though alarmed, it is not confounded; but as a lively flame and burning torch, it forces its way upward and securely passes through all. If any man love, he knows what is the cry of this voice. For it is a loud cry in the ears of God, that ardent affection of the soul, when it says, "My God, object of my love, You are all mine, and I am all Yours."

When You are present, all things are delightful, but when You are absent, all things are loathsome. You make a quiet heart and great peace and festal joy. You make us to think well of all circumstances and in all to praise You; neither can anything please long without You. But if it must needs be pleasant and of a good savor, Your grace must be present, and it must be seasoned with the seasoning of Your wisdom. What will not be of good savor unto him to whom You savor well? And him to whom You savor not, what shall have power to please?

Oh, how great a peace and quietness
would he possess who did cut off all vain anxiety
and think only upon divine things and such
as are profitable for his soul and place all his hope in God!

What can the world profit you without Jesus? To be without Jesus is a grievous hell; and to be with Jesus, a sweet paradise.

Jesus has now many lovers of His heavenly kingdom but few bearers of His cross. Many He has who are desirous of consolation but few of tribulation. Many He finds who share His table but few His fasting. All desire to rejoice with Him; few are willing to endure anything for Him. Many follow Jesus unto the breaking of bread but few to the drinking of the cup of His passion. Many reverence His miracles, while few follow the shame of His cross. Many love Jesus as long as no adversities befall them. Many praise and bless Him as long as they receive any consolation from Him. But if Jesus hide Himself and leave them but a little while, they fall either into complaining or into dejection of mind.

But they who love Jesus for the sake of Jesus, and not for some special comfort of their own, bless Him in all tribulation and anguish of heart, as well as in the highest comfort. Although He should never give them comfort, they would ever praise Him notwithstanding and wish to always give thanks. Oh, how powerful is the pure love of Jesus, which is mixed with no self-interest or self-love!

Never read a word that you may appear more learned....

I am He who, in one instant, does lift up the humble mind to comprehend more reasonings of eternal truth than if one had studied ten years in the schools.

I teach without noise of words, without confusion of opinions, without the pride of honor, without the scuffling of arguments.

To some men I speak common things; to others, things special. To some I show Myself sweetly in signs and figures, while to some I reveal mysteries in much light. The voice of books is one, but it informs not all alike. Inwardly, I am the teacher, the truth, the searcher of the heart, the discerner of thoughts, the promoter of actions, distributing to every man as I shall judge fit.

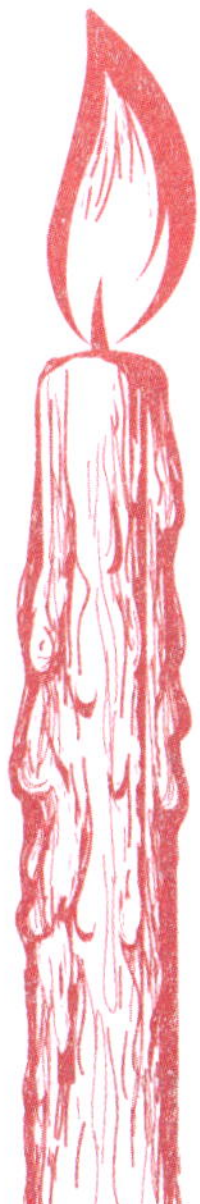

Love Him, and keep Him for your friend,
who, when all go away,
will not forsake you nor suffer you to perish in the end.
Sometime or other,
you must be separated from all,
whether you will it or not.
Keep close to Jesus both in life and in death,
and commit yourself unto His faithfulness who,
when all fail, can alone help you.

Your Beloved is of that nature that He will admit of no rival but will have your heart alone and sit on His throne as King....

You shall quickly be deceived if you only look to the outward appearance of men. For if in others you seek your comfort and profit, you shall too often feel loss. If you seek in all things Jesus, you shall surely find Jesus. But if you seek yourself, you shall also find yourself, but to your own destruction. For man is more hurtful to himself if he seeks not Jesus than the whole world and all its adversaries.

It is great skill to know how to hold converse with Jesus;
and to know how to keep Jesus,
great wisdom.
Be humble and peaceable,
and Jesus will be with you.
Be devout and quiet, and Jesus will stay with you.

My son, says the Lord, be not wearied by the labors that you have undertaken for my sake, nor let tribulations cast you down. But let My promise strengthen and comfort you under every circumstance. I am well able to reward you, above all measure and degree.

Know for certain that you ought to lead a dying life.
And the more any man dies to himself,
so much the more he begins to live unto God.

Behold, my God and my all! What can I desire more and what happier thing can I long for? O sweet and delicious Word!

Love is a great thing, yes, altogether a great good; it makes light everything that is heavy, and it bears evenly all that is uneven. For it carries a burden that is no burden and makes every bitter thing sweet and tasteful. The noble love of Jesus drives a man to do great things and stirs him to always long for what is more perfect. Love wills to be on high and not to be kept back by anything low and mean. Love wills to be free and estranged from all worldly affection so its inward sight may not be hindered, that it may not be entangled by any temporal prosperity or by any adversity subdued.

Most merciful Jesus, grant to me Your grace, that it may be with me, and labor with me, and persevere with me even to the end.

Grant me always to desire and to will that which is to You most acceptable. Let Your will be mine, and let my will ever follow Yours and agree perfectly with it. Let my will be one with Yours, and let me not be able to will or not to will anything else but what You will or will not.

...Grant to me, above all things that can be desired, to rest in You, and in You to have my heart at peace. You are the true peace of the heart; You its only rest; out of You, all things are hard and restless. In this peace, in this selfsame thing, that is, in You, the chiefest eternal good, I will sleep and rest.

Let my sighs move You and my manifold desolation here on earth, O Jesus, You brightness of the eternal glory, You comfort of the pilgrim soul. With You my tongue is without voice, and my very silence speaks to You. How long does my Lord delay to come? Let Him come to me, His poor despised servant, and make me glad. Let Him put forth His hand and deliver me in my misery from all anguish. Come, oh come; for without You no day or hour shall be glad; for You are my gladness, and without You my table is empty. In misery am I, and in a manner imprisoned and loaded with fetters, until You refresh me with the light of Your presence, and grant me liberty, and show a friendly countenance toward me. Let others seek what else they please instead of You; but for me, nothing else meanwhile pleases nor shall please me but You only, my God, my hope, my everlasting salvation. I will not hold my peace, nor cease to pray, until Your grace return again, and You speak inwardly to me.

O Lord Jesus, forasmuch as Your way was narrow and despised by the world, grant me grace to imitate You, though with the world's contempt. *"The disciple is not above his master, nor the servant above his lord"* (Matthew 10:24).

It shall perish altogether,
whatever is not born of God.

Come, brethren, we go forward together; Jesus will be with us. For the sake of Jesus, we have received this cross; for the sake of Jesus, let us persevere in the cross. He will be our Helper, who is also our Guide and Forerunner. Behold, our King enters in before us, and He will fight for us. Let us follow courageously; let no man fear any terrors. Let us be ready to die valiantly in battle, nor bring such disgrace on our glory as to flee from the cross.

Without You, I cannot be, and without Your visitation, I have no power to live. And therefore I must often draw near unto You, and obtain from You the medicine of my salvation; lest I faint in the way if I be deprived of the heavenly nourishment. For so, most merciful Jesus, You once did say, preaching to the people and curing various sicknesses: *"I will not send them away fasting, lest they faint in the way"* (Matthew 15:32). Deal, therefore, in like manner now with me.

Whatever is wanting in me,
O Jesus, most holy Savior,
do You in my behalf bountifully
and graciously supply,
You who have vouchsafed to
call us all unto You, saying,
"Come unto me,
all ye that labour and
are heavy laden,
and I will give you rest"
(Matthew 11:28).

Who is there that, approaching humbly unto a fountain of sweetness, does not carry away some little sweetness? Or who, standing near a great fire, receives not some small heat therefrom? And You are a fountain always full and overflowing; a fire ever burning and never going out. Wherefore, if I am not permitted to draw out of the fullness of the fountain, nor to drink my fill, I will, notwithstanding, set my lips to the mouth of this heavenly conduit, that I may receive from thence at least some small drop to refresh my thirst and may not wither. And though I cannot as yet be altogether heavenly, nor so on fire as the cherubim and seraphim, yet, notwithstanding, I will endeavor to apply myself earnestly to devotion and to prepare my heart to obtain but some small flame of divine fire.

Let all people, nations,
and languages praise You
and magnify Your holy name
with exultation and burning devotion.